Footprints In The
Sands Of Longwood

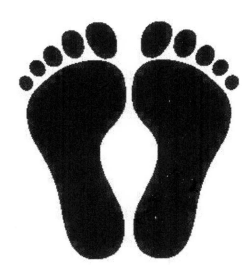

The Museum Committee
Central Florida Society For Historic Preservation
2014

Footsteps in Longwood History

This book is dedicated to John Bistline, a founding member of the Central Florida Society for Historic Preservation (CFSHP), who is the driving and creative force behind its creation.

Special thanks are given to Carolyn Bistline for her many efforts and contributions to its creation.

We also remember Jean and Ray McWilliams for their many years of service to the CFSHP, its Museum Committee, and the preparation of this book.

Final preparation of this book was done by the Museum Committee whose current members are: Chair, Marla Picklesimer, Secretary, Linda Stearns, and members Susan Hudson, Kathryn Goshen and Edwin Campbell.

While every effort has been made to be correct, this book should not be used as a direct source for any scholarly effort.

Section I

1860 – 1880

Many of the natural attractions of the area that would leave big footprints in Longwood's history were already here when a few pioneer families moved into the area. One of these pioneers was E. W. Henck who chose a part of this area to homestead and try to sell building lots. By 1880 he had established a post office and become aware that a town without easy transportation to the outside world would not sell. By the end of 1880, he and other investors raised capital and built a railroad from Sanford on the St. Johns River to Orlando. With access to river traffic he would see his town experience rapid growth.

Articles

1. The Senator
2. Hoosier/Sanlando Springs
3. Palm Springs and Shepherds (Starbucks) Springs
4. The Lee J. Hartley Family
5. Edward Warren Henck
6. John Neill Searcy
7. J. P. Clouser

The Senator

In January 2012, a fire resulting from a deliberate and thoughtless act of arson tragically destroyed the oldest existing tourist attraction in Central Florida. The cypress tree known as "The Senator" and often referred to simply as the "Big Tree" certainly predated Walt Disney World and other current attractions. The Senator was located in Big Tree Park in Seminole County's Spring Hammock Preserve, a small preserve in Longwood between Sanford and Orlando. Its younger companion, Lady Liberty, still stands nearby. The Senator, as the elder of the two, was thought to have been on the site for over 3,500 years. "Lady Liberty" is younger and probably started growing when Jesus walked the Earth.

For generations, tourists and locals alike enjoyed the marvel of two trees of this age and size still growing in the middle of 21st Century Florida.

This area of Seminole County was once thick with bay, sweet gum, live oaks, longleaf yellow pines, and cypress hammocks scattered with low swampland. The land changed little with the yearly progression of seasons. As described in 1881 by Maryland lawyer George W. Newell writing for the *Baltimore Sun* from Clifton Springs, a steamboat landing on the south shore of Lake Jessup: the land had altered little since coastal tribes followed the meandering St. Johns River inland. Thousands of years ago these tribes used the towering bald cypress to find their way to trading grounds. Shorn of its top by a long ago storm, the majestic tree was visible from the river eight miles away. In a version of modern day landfills, the first indigenous settlers built mounds or middens, piling sand, shells, and debris to create higher ground as they migrated inland in summer to hunt and trade. Winters for these ancient people were spent along the coast. Middens were additionally used for stilt homes or signal points between Lake Monroe and the interior settlements. (Some historians believe that the nearby Seminole County Museum sitting on just such a rise may be located on an ancient midden.)

During the Seminole wars in the mid 1800's, soldiers from nearby forts at Maitland, Harney, and Monroe searched for Seminoles throughout the region. Still much of the territory remained a remote wilderness until after the Civil War. Only then did settlement of the areas between Orlando and Sanford begin. A surveyor, J.O. Fries traveled the area in 1871 and noted a single lone house along the entire road. He saw one small store in Maitland.

In more recent times, the America Forestry Association in 1946 estimated that The Senator was just a seedling when Columbus set sail for what he hoped would be a short route to India. It easily predated occupation by Seminoles, the Spanish, the English, and the United States. In 1929, President Calvin Coolidge traveled to the area to stand dwarfed in its shade to praise it as a national treasure being, of course, one of the nation's oldest and largest trees.

Coolidge's visit was initiated when, in 1927, the Big Tree Park site was donated to Seminole County after the death of its owner, State Senator M.O. Overstreet . The

Overstreet family, starting with Ben J. Overstreet, owner of the Overstreet Turpentine Co., were major landowners during the lumber and turpentine era. The donation from Senator Overstreet clearly led to the big cypress's often used nickname, The Senator.

In 2013, a clone, genetically the same as the Big Tree, was installed at a renovated Big Tree Park. The clone had been growing since the 1990s when an orchard of seven Big Tree cuttings was planted in north Florida. Fittingly, the clone has been named "The Phoenix" after the mythical bird that rises from the ashes. Two sections of the original tree, one showing the blackened inside and the other the bark, are on display at the Museum of Seminole County History.

Unknowing of the Senator's eventual tragic fate, a visitor once wrote, " Reluctantly you leave the big tree's stately presence. But you know that any time you yearn for a quick escape and serenity, The Senator will still be waiting."

Sources: *Flashbacks: The Story of Central Florida's Past, Longwood* , floridagardner.com, wildemeories.com, floridahikes.com

The Springs

Hoosier/Sanlando Springs

This was known as Hoosier Springs from the days of the early settlers in the 1870's. The spring, about 4.5 miles west of Longwood pours out gallons of clear, 72 degree water year round. It is the southernmost of 3 springs: Sanlando, Palm and Starbucks, that lie along the Little Wekiva River for a distance of about one half mile. Sanlando Springs is located about 500 feet north of where S. R. 434 crosses the Little Wekiva River.

All of the water from the spring emptied into the coffee colored Little Wekiva River which ran along one edge of the pool. The coffee color comes from the palmetto roots growing along the river's edge. The cool waters of the springs were greatly appreciated by the nearby residents during hot summer months. A wagon trail led from Longwood to Apopka and passed by the springs. By 1887 there was a Florida Midland R. R. station within easy walking distance.

Life in Florida changed rapidly during the boom times of the 1920's. Subdivisions sprang up in Longwood and Altamonte Springs. In 1924, on the north side of his Altamonte subdivision, Mr. Frank Haithcox purchased a large parcel of land from Moses Overstreet which included Hoosier Springs. Mr. Haithcox proceeded to develop the springs into an area attraction by enclosing one side of the pool with a cement walk including steps leading down to the pool. He made the pool larger by damming up the springs which also eliminated the brown river water. He created a lawn area on the slope leading to the spring. He then created a separate swimming pool filled daily with fresh spring water by means of a pumping station. In 1926 ground was broken for a 50 room hotel, but it was never built. The pool house contained a few slot machines which were gone by 1930. Also in the pool house was the ubiquitous Coca Cola ice box containing not only Coke but also Ne-High and Orange Crush sodas. Use of the grounds was free and the only charge was for the bath house and pool. Renamed Sanlando Springs, it quickly gained recognition as the playground of Central Florida. In 1926, Warren Street in Longwood was extended west to Sanlando Springs. The extension followed the road bed of the now defunct Florida Midland R. R. as does S. R. 434 today.

When the Florida land boom broke and was quickly followed by the depression of the 1930's, the property reverted to Moses Overstreet who undertook extensive changes to the spring area and the building surrounding the pool. Renamed Sanlando Springs Tropical Park, the Little Wekiva River was diverted around the spring area allowing a large sandy area to be created. The area between the sand and the diverted river was landscaped with azaleas and shallow pools containing water lilies of various colors. On the high ground above the spring, a terrazzo dance floor was constructed and speakers placed in the overhanging branches of a large oak tree provided the music. Once again the park became immensely popular throughout Central Florida. During the years of the second world war, large busses brought GI's from area bases to the Park.

In 1950, Mr. and Mrs. J. E. Robinson bought the park and continued to make improvements. In 1970, the park was closed and the land was acquired by the gated Springs subdivision. The spring area is now only open to the public when the popular Springs Concert is given there by the Orlando Symphony Orchestra as a fund raiser.

Palm Springs and Shepherds (Starbucks) Springs

Palm Springs is the middle spring of the trio that lies along the Wekiva River on the west side of Markham Woods road and just north of S. R. 434. Palm Springs is the only one of the trio not bordered by the river which is approximately 200 yards distant. As a result it forms a clear pool of water unlike the other 2 which are coffee colored by the water from the Little Wekiva River. The clear pool was the first choice of early settlers.

Improvements were made over the years and by the mid-teens of the 20th century it was in use by local residents and residents and guests at the Altamonte Springs Hotel.

In the early 1920's, Palm Springs underwent further renovation when Lester Beeman of the chewing gum family, who was at that time an Orlando businessman, and several others built cottages there. It became a popular bathing spot for area residents.

Its popularity waned in the 1930's and in 1944 Moses Overstreet purchased the property with the intention of combining the area with his Sanlando Springs Tropical Park. However, this was never accomplished.

Shepherds Springs is located about 2200 feet further north and on the west side of the river. Surrounded by a thick upland hammock, it was never developed. The Little Wekiva River is adjacent to the spring so the pool of clear water is limited. Shepherds Springs was reached by a road from Wekiva Springs Road and was a picturesque spot for picnics. It was also used for overnight camping by the Boy Scouts. The original name is thought to have come from a family named Shepherd living in that area. The name was changed to Starbucks when the spring became part of the Springs subdivision.

All three springs are located within what is now The Springs gated subdivision and therefore not available to the public.

The Lee J. Hartley Family

Mr. & Mrs. Lee J. Hartley and their 4 children were already established pioneers when Mr. Henck came to the area in 1872. The Hartley's had staked out a 160 acre homestead south of Lake Wildmere and west of Fairy Lake down to about what today is Dog Track Road. They had come to Longwood from northern Florida and had planted a citrus grove of Satsuma oranges. Their land grant is dated November 30, 1878 and is signed by President Rutherford B. Hayes.

In 1992, a number of Mr. Hartley's journals were found in an old abandoned desk in one of his son's home. The journals provide an interesting insight into farming practices and prices in the area from 1888 to 1912. In addition to orange groves, Mr. Hartley had a truck farm and ran a commissary in the 1880's. His business was known as Fairy Lake Farm which sold produce locally and even shipped some to New York City. The journals are now in the archives of the George A. Smathers Library at the University of Florida.

Some extracts gleaned from the journals include:

On September 4, 1911 a man made 94 cents working 7.5 hours "covering peas and sprouting trees." A full work day was 10 hours which the man worked for the remainder of the month at a daily wage of $1.25 hoeing, haying and "sprouting trees."

On February 28, 1912 Mr. Hartley reported shipments of oranges to New York City. He received $178.05 for 156 boxes. He also noted that "There is nothing in raising cotton. I sold 800 pounds a few days ago for $.05 per pound. The beauty about trucking is if you get your Irish potatoes and beans in early they will come off in time for you to plant the same ground in corn and sweet potatoes."

The commissary was run in connection with the truck farm. Items sold and the prices but not the quantity are listed. Cider was listed as $.05, $.10, $.15 and $.25. Bacon was sold for $.25 and $.31. A side note indicates that the train fare to Sanford was $.80 but doesn't say if that was one way or round trip.

Mr. Hartley also had some cattle a few of which wandered into an oncoming South Florida Train. The company was held responsible and settled in the price range of $10 to $35.

In the early 1900's the Hartley's operated a grove care business in the area. One of the sons, William, operated a grocery store in the former bank section of the business block located at the junction of S.R. 427 and Church Street during the 1930's and 1940's.

Edward Warren Henck

To quote the historical marker located in Longwood, "Mr. E.W. Henck, a young man of Boston, arrived in this wilderness section of then Orange County in November of 1872" (Seminole County was not separated from Orange County until 1913.) Mr. Henck had arrived by steamboat in Sanford, then called Mellonville, on the St. Johns River. He walked overland to what is now the Historic Longwood Area where he and his wife staked out an approximately one hundred and sixty acre homestead claim on mostly high and dry land in the public domain. They occupied it in a tent until they could build a home. On June 24, 1878 they became owners of the land.

An engineer by background, Mr. Henck laid out the area and named it Longwood after a grand estate named Longwood on which he had worked in the Brookline suburb of Boston. The estate in turn had been named after the estate on St. Helena Island in the South Atlantic, off Africa, to which Napoleon was ultimately exiled. His town was bounded by Orange Ave. on the north, West Lake St. (now Milwee) on the west, Grant Ave. on the East and Molnar St. on the south (now SR 434). Most lots were 50 x 100 ft.

In 1876, he was named the first Postmaster of Longwood. On March 16, 1880, Mr. Henck deeded the land bounded by East Lake on the east, Church Street on the South, a strip of land 200 ft. wide and 1350 ft. long (about 6 acres), to the Episcopal Diocese of Florida. Later, in April 1885 the Diocese deeded back to Mr. Henck the strip of land 200 ft. wide starting on East Lake and running west 200 ft. along Church St. Mr. Henck also donated land on Pine St. to the Corinth Missionary Baptist Church.

To encourage growth, Mr. Henck along with Mr. Haskell of Maitland began a railroad to run between Sanford and Orlando. The South Florida Railroad started running in 1880; and the present tracks running through Longwood are on the road bed laid out for the South Florida Railroad. Mr. Henck eventually sold his railroad to the Henry Plant Rail System.

Longwood was incorporated as a town in 1883 and Mr. Henck was elected the first mayor. Longwood maps of 1886 show the Florida Midland Railroad running through town on Florida Avenue and a spur of the Orange Belt railroad running down Bay St. from the west to Mr. Demens' lumber mill located in the block between Warren and Bay Streets and centered across Myrtle Avenue. By 1887, Mr. Henck's Longwood boasted a population of over 1000.

The first Longwood Hotel is identified on the "Birds Eye View of Longwood" published in 1885 as being on the east side of the railroad with a Mr. Henry Hand as proprietor. Mr. Henck desired a much more imposing hotel to set off his growing town and began a second three story hotel known as the Waltham. It was completed in 1888. In full view of the passengers riding the railroad cars, it had 38 rooms. It is still standing and is now known as the Longwood Village Inn operating as an office building.

Although recent historians could not find conclusive proof, Mr. Henck alleged that he had been a member of the honor guard on the train which returned President Lincoln's body to Illinois.

Mr. Henck died in 1930.

EDWARD WARREN HENCK

John Neill Searcy

Like E. W. Henck, Mr. Searcy also arrived in Mellonville (Sanford) by steamboat and began homesteading in the Longwood area in 1873. Mr. Searcy was originally from Tennessee and had served in the Confederate army as a sergeant during the Civil War.

At some point, Mr. Searcy's father, John, who was a doctor, joined him in Longwood and they, with several other prominent citizens, helped build the Christ Episcopal Church on West Church Street which was dedicated in 1882. The land for the church was donated by E. W. Henck.

In 1885, he married Eva Lessie Muzzy. Together they had 3 sons, only one of whom survived until adulthood. Mr. Searcy was a carpenter, worked on a railroad survey crew, planted groves and served as Postmaster in Longwood for several years beginning in 1889.

In 1888, he built a Victorian home at 593 West Church Street which still stands and is now known as Magnolia Acres.

Eva Searcy

J. B. Clouser

J.B. Clouser was a 7th generation descendent of Hans Jarick Clouser who arrived in Philadelphia on September 11, 1728 from the Palentine Region of Germany. He and his family settled in Bucks County, Pennsylvania.

J.B. was born in Perry County, Pennsylvania on October 15, 1838. Raised on a farm he chose the trade of a carpenter. He enlisted on the northern side in the Civil War as a member of the 149 P.B. Company D. Buck Tails. After his discharge he resumed the carpenter trade. He was married in November 1868 to Elizabeth Clouser, his cousin, and established a home in Center Township, Perry County, Pennsylvania.

In 1881, he answered an advertisement for a master carpenter placed in a northern paper by Mr. Henck, founder of Longwood. The position was to supervise the construction of a hotel in Orange County, Florida in a settlement known as Longwood. Mr. Henck needed a hotel visible from trains passing through the village as a sign that it was a growing town.

When the Clouser family (his wife Elizabeth, son, Charles 18 and daughter, Francis, age 13) arrived in Longwood in November 1881, there was no suitable place for them to live. He quickly built the Clouser Cottage on Church Street, followed a couple of years later by his larger house on Warren Avenue. After completing the construction of the Longwood Hotel (now the Longwood Village Inn), he took a job with P.A. Demens Co. as foreman of their novelty and lumber planing mill, at that time the only such mill south of Jacksonville. After four years he left the employment of the P.A. Demens Co. to join with his son Charles A. and his son-in-law, F.J. Niemeyer to open a mercantile business on Lake St. in Longwood. He retired from the business when his wife died in 1911. He then became a cabinet maker. His son, Charles, moved to New Smyrna where he was in the automobile business. Mr. F. J. Niemeyer carried on the business under the name of F.J. Niemeyer.

Mr. Clouser was active in the civic affairs of Longwood, being elected an Alderman on the first City Council in 1883. He served as mayor in 1889, 1895 and 1903. He was one of the founders of the Longwood Cemetery Association which established the cemetery on North Grant Street. He died on March 6. 1920.

In 2001, the State of Florida honored Mr. J.B Clouser as one of the Great Floridians in their "Great Floridians" 2000 Marker Program.

Note 1: In 2000 when his army record became available on the Internet, it was discovered that at the time Mr. Clouser enlisted he gave his occupation as watch maker. At the time of his death his request for health benefits still listed his occupation as watch maker.
Note 2. Much of the information used here can be found in "Early Settlers of Orange County, CE Howard, Publisher, Orlando, Florida, 1915, and in an unpublished document: "Descendents of Elizabeth (Clouser) Dyle" compiled by her granddaughter, Mary L. (Clegg) Schmoker.

Section II

1880 – 1895

During this era, Longwood experienced a rapid growth. From as few as 50 residents in the general area in 1881, the population was listed as over 1000 in 1888. Several factors played a big part. The Peter Demens saw mill grew quickly. With abundant pine and cypress trees nearby and railroad access at his door, he supplied building material for hotels rising along the railroad from Sanford to Tampa.

Locally, citrus trees planted in the area came into production and settlers were attracted to the area. With a ready market, businesses appeared in Longwood.

Terminating in Longwood, The Florida Midlands railway ran west toward Apopka and connected with the Orange Belt Railway at Palm Springs Junction. With the addition of the second railroad, Longwood became a shopping destination for a large area.

The great freezes of December 1894 and February 1895 nearly brought an end to a thriving town.

Articles

1. Peter Demens
2. List of Businesses
3. West Longwood
4. South Florida Railroad
5. Florida Midland Railway
6. Orange Bely Railway
7. Christ Episcopal Church
8. Corinth-Olive Missionary Church
9. First Baptist Church
10. Longwood Elementary School
11. The Big Freeze

Peter Demens

Mr. Demens arrived in Longwood in 1881 when he was 31 years old. He was born into Russian nobility as Pyotr Alekseyevich Dementyev and served for a time as an officer in the Imperial Guards. An orphan, he inherited his estates at an early age but apparently had little success with them and decided to emigrate to America.

Upon arrival in Longwood, he had sufficient funds to purchase 80 acres for an orange grove and a one-third interest in a sawmill. According to his personal account, he worked laboriously to clear the land for orange trees and to assist in the sawmill, eventually buying out his less industrious partners.

He grew the business into a major supplier of building materials in the area and expanded it to include design and construction as well. One of his contracts was to supply railroad ties for the infant Orange Belt Railroad. When the railroad could not pay for them, Mr. Demens was presented with the charter instead. When he acquired the line, it had a charter to run from the St. Johns River to Lake Apopka. Mr. Demens spent his energies during the next several years raising the capital and expanding the line to its ultimate terminus in St. Petersburg, Florida.

Mr. Demens served as mayor of Longwood and in 1884 was an unsuccessful candidate for the state senate.

To satisfy his debts, Mr. Demens sold the railroad in 1889 and moved to North Carolina. He died in California in 1919.

Business Owners Who Made Longwood,
But Whose Footprints, The Sands of Time Have Erased

Dr. Norman, Drugs
A.M. Taylor & Co., Groceries
Jas. R. Poole   "
E. E. Petris   "
Park & Ball   "
E. Molnar, Bakery and Groceries
B. E. Phelfner, Laundry
R. J. Reid   "
G. L. Takach, Restaurant
J. Hand, Hotel
W. A. Simmons, Butcher
J. Thompson, Butcher
H. Hand, Livery Stable
W. Smith, Blacksmith and Wagon Maker
B. Wright, Confectionary
B. Wright, Barber
Longwood News, C.V. Wilson, Editor/Proprietor
        (published every Saturday)
Mrs. L. Davis, Millinery and fancy goods
South Florida Lightning Rod Company
King, Miller and Hall, Real Estate and Surveyors
P. A. Demens & Company

West Longwood

West Longwood was the name of a social entity of families living on the west wide of Mr. Henck's town of Longwood in the 1880's to sometime around 1910. The east side of West Longwood apparently began with the families living on the south side of Greenwood Lake (now West Lake) about where present day Church Street makes a westerly bend out to Rangeline Road, and included all the families living in the area west of there. This area started to build up around 1880. Families were probably attracted to the area as the soil was good for citrus and they needed a larger plot of land than was available in the town.

It can be deduced from the Longwood Social Notes in the Jacksonville Times Union of this era, that several of these families came from Natick, Mass., as it was reported in 1888 there was the suggestion that the area name be changed from West Longwood to Nova Natick.

Sometime in the 1880's, these families acquired the first Longwood town meeting building that is reported to have been built in the area where Christ Episcopal Church now stands. When it was built and by whom is not known. It was a large one room building with an elegant rounded barrel type ceiling. It was moved to the area where Church Street meets Rangeline Road.

Often referred to as the West Longwood Chapel, it became the home of the West Longwood Pioneers and Self Union. The May 10, 1892 entry in the Longwood News published in the Jacksonville Times Union relates--"For some ten years past, ladies of the town, now called West Longwood, have given a monthly social consisting of both vocal and instrumental music, recitals, plays, etc., ending up with coffee and cake. These socials have been held in the Union Chapel at West Longwood and have always been pleasant affairs."

Interest in maintaining the organization waned after the turn of the century and the West Longwood Chapel was sold to the Longwood Civic League Organization. In 1912, it was moved back to its present location on Church Street. At that time, additions in the form of a front porch and two wings on either end of the chapel were added. In 1999, it was deeded to the Central Florida Society for Historic Preservation and is now known as the Longwood Historic Civic Center.

South Florida Railroad

The South Florida Railroad was incorporated on October 16, 1878 by E. W. Henck, E.F. Crafts, H. Mercer, and Dr. C.C. Haskell, all of Orange County, Florida. These men hired F. C. Tucker as chief engineer and he located a line running from Lake Monroe (on the St. Johns River) at Sanford to Orlando. The road was projected to run all the way down the state to Charlotte Harbor on the Gulf of Mexico. The South Florida RR was having trouble raising money, but when Mr. Henck obtained the charter of the defunct LM&O, the project was able to go forward.

E.W. Henck had a special reason for wanting to build this railroad. Coming to the area in 1873 from Boston, Henck homesteaded a site near Mrytle Lake which he platted as a small village. He named the village Longwood after a suburb of Boston he had helped to lay out. He knew that if he was to sell lots in Longwood and the town was to prosper, reliable rail transportation into the area from Sanford would be essential.

Mr.Henck was able to convince two prominent investors from Boston that a railroad from Sanford to Orlando, and then onward to the gulf through a new and undeveloped Florida, was a solid investment. Henck was made president of the railroad. Traveling back to Florida he made purchases of ten miles of rail and a little narrow gauge locomotive. Construction began with ex-president U.S. Grant throwing the first shovel of dirt. Despite this grand beginning, actual progress was slow as labor was hard to come by in the undeveloped region. The little locomotive "Seminole" along with 75 tons of rail arrived at Sanford by the end of January 1880. By May 20th, seven miles of iron had been laid to Shroder's Mill. This increased to nineteen miles by the first of July, leaving only three miles left to reach Orlando.

Unfortunately by then, the South Florida's supply of rails had been exhausted, and because of the railroad building boom in the country, there would be a three-month lull in completing the road to Orlando. To make the most of this delay, Henck began construction of the Lake Monroe-St. Johns River wharf at Sanford. The wharf was 800 feet long and could accommodate five steamboats at a time.

Finally the rails arrived in October and the last three miles were quickly laid. The first public timetable was issued on November 11, 1880. The Longwood station was on the south side of Church Street. There was a passenger entrance as well as a large area for freight shipments. Later, the "porch stand" was used for watching the Longwood baseball team play in the field next to the tracks.

The railroad still only owned the little "Seminole". She hauled the north bound train leaving Orlando at 7:00 AM and arrived in Sanford at 8:40 AM. After switching in Sanford for most of the day the "Seminole" became the southbound train, departing Sanford at 4:00 PM, tying up for the night in Orlando at 5:40 PM.

In December of 1880, Mr. Henck was ousted because of the construction delays. With his replacement, gone also was his determination to build to the gulf coast. There followed a period of several changes in philosophy about the direction and extension of the construction of the railroad. By March of 1882, rail was completed to Kissimmee. Plans again were to construct from there to Tampa. At this time, the South Florida Railroad was the southern most railroad in the United States.

By the end of 1882, the South Florida owned five small wood burning narrow gauge locomotives. Other equipment consisted of five coaches, two combination mail, baggage and express cars, fifteen box cars and twenty flat cars. All the freight equipment was only 25 feet in length and had capacity of only 15,000 lbs. The timetable in 1882 consisted of four trains, two passenger trains and two mix trains. No trains were run on Sundays

Tampa of 1883 was a town in decline, steadily losing population and in need of a railroad. Situated on the best harbor on the gulf coast, the first railroad there would reap vast riches from the potential growth of the port and would have control of shipping on the Gulf of Mexico to the West Indies within their grasp. Also there was the reward of vast amounts of land being offered by the State of Florida for the first railroad to enter Tampa.

On May 4, 1883, Henry B. Plant and his Plant System (headed by the Savannah, Florida and Western (SF&W) Railway) bought 3/5 of the stock of the South Florida after an unsuccessful attempt to buy the Florida Southern Railway. Plant had made an agreement with the Florida Southern not to build the SF&W south of Gainesville or Palatka, the northern ends of the Florida Southern, but the existing South Florida was immune from this. Plant then made agreements with all the railroads building towards Tampa except for the Florida Transit and Peninsular Railroad. Specifically, the Florida Southern would not build any lines south of Pemberton's Ferry and Brooksville or north of Bartow, and the South Florida would build their Pemberton Ferry Branch between the two and assign trackage rights to the Florida Southern. The agreement with the Jacksonville, Tampa and Key West (JTK&R) Railway specified that that company would only build north of Sanford; in both cases the South Florida would give up their rights to the territories given to the other companies. The JT&KW had already done some grading at Bartow and Tampa, and sold them to the South Florida.

Thus two railroads remained on a race towards Tampa - the South Florida and the Florida Transit and Peninsular Railroad. The South Florida managed to get there first, and obtained the best ports (now known as Port Tampa). The Tampa end opened on December 10, 1883, and on January 25, 1884 service began over the full line, built to three-foot (914 mm) narrow gauge. On February 20, 1886 the standard-gauge Jacksonville, Tampa and Key West Railway opened to Sanford, and the South Florida was converted to standard gauge on September 22.

In 1893, the Savannah, Florida and Western Railway (Plant System) directly acquired the South Florida. In 1902, the Atlantic Coast Line Railroad acquired the Plant System, and in 1967 the ACL merged into the Seaboard Coast Line Railroad. The line eventually passed to CSX, and now operates as part of one of its two main lines in the area, known as the "A" Line.

Florida Midland Railway

The men and boys of 1899 Longwood extinguished the fire. It is September 30, 1899 and a railroad depot platform has been set ablaze by sparks from a northbound freight train. Increasing the danger, east winds carry sparks to nearby buildings. After the danger has passed, prominent resident Fred Niemeyer returns to his home a quarter mile from the fire and prepares for bed. On the covers he finds a piece of charred shingle from the depot, apparently carried there by the wind. Seemingly, the small village of Longwood has escaped a very real chance of a much greater catastrophe than the loss of only several buildings near the depot.

The depot involved in this fire was part of the Florida Midland Railway (FMR). The Florida Midland Railway Company was originally incorporated under the general incorporation laws of Florida, and reincorporated on February 10, 1885 at which time only 10 miles had been graded. The new owners were E. W. Henck (founder of Longwood), S. M. Breuster, Carl Cushing, A. Menser and C. E. Munson of Florida, and Edward Page, Charles W. Morris and Cyrus Carpenter of Boston, Massachusetts.

The route of the Midland was to start on the Indian River in Brevard County and run to a point on the Gulf of Mexico. Permission to cross the South Florida line was not granted requiring the abandonment of the section of the line from the south shore of Lake Jessup. The line actually built ran from Longwood west to Apopka and then turning south to Kissimmee.

Stations listed from north to south were to include:

- Clifton [The FMR was unable to obtain permission from the South Florida RR to cross the their tracks in Longwood, making completion of this station unnecessary]
- Longwood (junction South Florida Railroad)
- Palm Springs (junction Orange Belt Railway)
- Lake Brantley
- Fitzville
- East Apopka (junction Apopka and Clay Spring Railway)
- Apopka (junction Florida Central and Peninsular Railroad Orlando Division)
- Clarcona (junction Orange Belt Railway)
- VillaNova
- Ocoee (junction Tavares, Apopka and Gulf Railroad)
- Minorville
- Gotha
- Windermere
- Doctor Phillips, previously known as Harperville
- Vineland, previously known as Orange Center, also Englewood
- Molanes
- Shingle Creek (Shingle PO)
- Kissimmee (junction South Florida Railroad)

As the tracks were laid and completed for the Florida Midland Railroad in the 1880's, growth in the area was rapid. Many more settlers moved in, large areas were cleared, and the market grew larger with better transportation facilities. Hard surfaced roads did not come until many years later, but the sand trails were improved. As a result, crops like corn, cotton, and sweet potatoes were abandoned in favor of more lucrative citrus groves and vegetables for the winter market of the north.

Perhaps foreshadowed by its difficult beginnings, the Florida Midland Railway was not destined to be long-lived. Insufficient business sent it into receivership from 1891 to 1896. At that point it suffered a similar fate of two other railroads in Central Florida and was sold to the Plant System. In 1902, the Atlantic Coast Line took over and the section between Longwood and Apopka was abandoned.

In more recent times, the Florida Midland Railroad was acquired from CSXT in 1987. FMID operates 28 miles of track on two separate branch lines that interchange with CSXT at Winter Haven, West Lake Wales, and Wildwood.

Today, from Clifton to Apopka, the railroad has been abandoned for about 100 years, and almost no traces are left. Parts of the right-of-way were used to construct SR 434.
From Apopka to Clarcona, the right-of-way is used for the West Orange Trail.
From Clarcona to Ocoee, the right-of-way is currently owned by CSX and run by the Florida Central Railroad. From Ocoee to Kissimmee, the railroad is abandoned, and some elements remain.

Christ Episcopal Church

Probably the first Sacrament of the Episcopal Church to be performed in the little community of Longwood was the baptism of the baby daughter of Mr. and Mrs. Frederick Rand. The child was baptized in their home on Easter Day 1877 by the Reverend J.H.M. Wendell, a young clergyman recently come to Florida from Middlebury, Vermont. The Rands decided to make Longwood their home and Mr. Rand, being appointed lay reader, read the service of the Church on Sundays in a small log school house on the property of E.W. Henck.

Mr. and Mrs. Edward Rand of Boston, Massachusetts, visiting their son in Longwood, became interested in the idea of building a church and upon going back to Boston, procured funds for the erection of the building. Mr. E.W. Henck, one of the earliest settlers of Longwood, had already given a plot of land for this purpose. Mr. Rand drew plans for the little Church and in 1889 with the help of the Reverend F.R. Holman, John and James Searcy (Longwood pioneers) and others, the Church was built. The consecration of the Church was celebrated on Easter Day, April 19, 1882 by the Reverend Lyman Phelps.

It is not known by whom they were given to Christ Church but the Communion Chalice, the silver Alms Basin, and the large old Bible, are all dated 1879. The beautiful stained, leaded glass window over the Altar was a gift of Mrs. Edward Rand of Boston. In 1880, a hurricane damaged Holy Cross Church in Sanford so badly that it was necessary to erect a new building. The congregation provided new furnishing for its new Holy Cross Church and so donated their old furnishing, still in good repair, to Christ Church. Thus the little Church received the wooden Altar, the Lectern and a carpet which was in use for many years. Mr. Albert Martin, a master cabinet maker from Natick, Massachusetts, made the reading desk which is still in use. The Baptismal Font made of several hundred pieces of native Florida wood was beautifully put together by F. H. Rand, J. B. Clouser and James Arnold.

The brass Altar vases and the Cross were given to the Church in 1884 by the F.H. Rand family in memory of Mr. and Mrs. Edward Rand and the Reverend Charles Rand all of whom were lost at sea on their way to Florida. The bell in the tower was given as a memorial to Mr. F.H. Rand's mother.

In 1883, the Mission Church in Longwood was in the charge of the Reverend F.H. Holman, who from that date until 1888 made his home in Longwood. He organized the Sunday school and did much to carry forward the work of Christ Church in the Longwood community. In the spring of 1887, The Right Reverend G. Wood, new Bishop of Florida, made his first visitation to Christ Church and confirmed one person. In 1889, the Mission of the Church was placed in the care of Reverend William H. Bates who had been the former headmaster of St. Paul's School, Concord, New Hampshire. Under Mr. Bates the influence of the Church increased greatly and fine work was carried on. The Church was completed and free of debt and the land and the building were placed in the keeping of the Diocese. The Right Reverend Edwin G. Wood, Bishop of Florida, consecrated Christ Church in that year, 1889. Mr. Bates started an Episcopal Parochial School for boys and girls and by 1901 the school found it necessary to erect a commodious dormitory for the increased enrollment of the boarding school students. Bad weather prevented the completion of the dormitory by the time the school opened on October 7, 1902. Unfortunately, Reverend Bates' health forced him to resign and he preached his last sermon the second Sunday in October of 1902.

Following the Reverend Bates' retirement various clergymen assumed charge of the Mission. Among them were the Reverend Mr. Greetham; Dean Lucian Spencer; Reverend Mr. Punnett; Reverend J.J. Bowker and the Reverend A.A. Rickert; Mr. Rand conducting a Lay Readers Service when no clergyman was available. In 1916, the Rand family moved to Orlando and for a number of years Mr. Rand continued to give his services as a Reader two Sundays a month when no clergyman was free to take charge.

From 1927 until 1945, the Mission of Christ Church was taken care of by several rectors from Holy Cross Church, Sanford and other clergymen who became available as needed. Around this time the original Record Book of the Mission of Christ Church was taken to Sanford for safe keeping and was thereby lost in the fire which destroyed Holy Cross Church and the Rectory in the early 1920s.

There were originally six oil lamps in the Church for lights. In 1955, Mrs. Janice Colle bought and gave eight more as she found them in shops all the way from Florida to Nova Scotia. They are lighted during the latter part of the midnight Mass on Christmas Eve but are more of a nostalgic reminder of other days than a help to sight.

The Parish House was erected in early 1958 and dedicated on June 5th of that year by Bishop Louttit. In 1963, plans were made for the enlargement and partial rebuilding of the Church. The Vestry and Congregation giving hearty approval, the plans were given to A.B. Williams Company of Winter Park, contractors and builders, by the Architect Robert Hammond of the congregation. In 1964, the newly built wings, which added much space to the nave of Christ Church, were dedicated.

The first annual Vacation Bible School in the Parish House began on Monday, July 13, 1964. The program called for daily sessions from 8:30 a.m. to 11:30 a.m. Monday through Friday for two weeks.

Sunday, June 6, 1965 saw the ground breaking for the new Educational Building with plans for at least four elementary grades. The rooms also were to be used on Sundays for Church School. The building was ready for use in September. There were now five classrooms and two offices, one for use of the church generally and the Vicar's private office. All are air conditioned as is the Church. This building was dedicated by Bishop Louttit on November 29th and was named Searcy Hall.

Later it was decided to move the sanctuary west from its 108 year resting place to a position in which the front entrance to the church was in line with the center of Wilma Street which dead ends on Church Avenue in front of the Church.

Starting around 1980 the Church has given a Lessons and Carols Service in partnership with the Central Florida Society for Historic Preservation for a "Victorian Christmas" program at the start of the Christmas Season.

Corinth-Mt. Olive Missionary Church

Organized in 1883, the Corinth Missionary Baptist Church is the second oldest church in Longwood, still holding services today. (Christ Episcopal Church held their first service in their new church in April of 1882). In both cases, Mr. Edward Henck, founder of Longwood in the 1870's, gave the parcels of land for the new churches: on West Church Street for the Episcopal Church and on West Pine Street, west of Longwoods's first school building on Wilma Avenue, for the Corinth Missionary Baptist Church.

Soon after platting his town in the 1880's, Mr. Henck realized the necessity of easy transportation to his new town if it was to prosper and was instrumental in bringing a railroad through Longwood from Sanford to Orlando and beyond. During this time, many Negroes came to the area in search of work. Some of them settled along the embankment of the railroad and built homes. A number of the pioneer families felt the need for a leader and a formal place of worship. They called the Rev. E.C. Jones to be their pastor, and approached Mr.Henck concerning their need. He gave them the small lot mentioned above, not far from the railroad track, with the stipulation that as long as the property was used as a place of worship, the title belonged to the church and this stipulation was included in his will. Together with the help of the congregation, and especially Brother Thomas Shepard, a church was soon constructed. The steeple contained a bell that was rung on Sunday mornings one half hour before and at the start of the service to summon the congregation. The church prospered under Pastor Jones' leadership.

Rev. Jones resigned in 1894 and the Rev. Charles J. Smith was called as Minister. He lived in Sanford and walked the railroad tracks each Sunday to preach. His salary was $8.00 a month and walking saved the the railroad fare.

At Mr. Henck's death, he left the property to Mrs. Barbara Jo Hunt, his secretary, and the agreement with the church was kept.

In later years, as the Longwood community grew, the white settlers built up around the church. They complained about the night services, and they were discontinued.

In 1942, Rev. Oliver Glover was called as pastor. During this time many people of different backgrounds were added to the church roll, and the members wanted to resume night services. Therefore, the Board of Deacons and the Trustees approached Mrs. Hunt and expressed their desire to move the church to a different location. With her consent the building was torn down. Two acres of land were purchased from Elder Charles Hines on SR 434, and a new building was erected. It was dedicated on April 3, 1965, and it was at this time that the church's name was changed to Mt. Olive Missionary Baptist Church. The congregation rejoiced to be able to worship whenever they wanted. The Rev. Glover's leadership lasted for 33 years. During this time a choir stand and bathrooms were added to the facility.

In 1975, Rev. Epps was called to be their new pastor. A new roof was put on the old section of the building and new pews were installed. The church helped organize the Island Lake Missionary Baptist Church.

In February 1987, Rev. Cannon C. Haynie was installed as minister and during his ministry, the church was painted inside and out; a pastor's office and study was added; their Bus Ministry was organized with the purchase of a van; their First Bible School convened; an organ was purchased and central air and heating was installed throughout the church. A Food and Clothing Bank was established.

Between 1989 and the present time, a number of pastors have enriched the spiritual lives of the members. In August of 2009, Mrs. Norweida Maxwell, the widow of the Rev. Dr. Fred L. Maxwell, who served as General Overseer from 2002 until his death in December 2005, was ordained and installed as pastor of the 126 year old Mt. Olive Missionary Baptist Church in Longwood. She became the first black woman pastor in the traditional black Missionary Baptist Church.

Mrs. Chaney Burnett Smith

Rev. Charles J. Smith

Rev. Oliver Glover and his wife, Maebelle Glover

First Baptist Church of Longwood

The First Baptist Church of Longwood was organized on May 31, 1891. With only fifteen members and less than $10.00 in receipts that year, it was indeed a very humble beginning for the young church. For the next 117 years, the church survived crises and experienced growth, all of which have shaped the church into what it is today, the body of Christ known as First Baptist Church of Longwood.

In the 1890's, all of Central Florida was traumatically impacted by a freeze that caused a major economic crisis. The church did not escape the effects of the crisis. For the most part, with the exception of informal gathering for prayer and fellowship, the church ceased to function and it appears that, for ten years, the church was inoperable.

By the turn of the century, the church began to grow slowly and was served by a circuit-riding minister. In 1933, the church voted to have preaching every week, which proved to be a catalyst for stabilization and growth. At this time there were 60 members on the church roll, and by 1940, there were 172. Ten years later the membership had grown to 224. During the 1950's the church continued to reach out and sponsor mission churches in Altamonte Springs, Lake Mary, and Deltona. In 1957, the Lake Mary mission was constituted into a church and the Altamonte Springs Chapel became the First Baptist Church of Altamonte Springs. Also in 1957, Longwood Baptist Church officially became the First Baptist Church of Longwood.

In the 1960's and 1970's membership continued to grow, doubling in the 1950's and leveling off in the late 1970's. In 1960, there were 353 members and by 1970, there were 760 members on the roll. It was during this time that Rev. Jack Lindsay, pastor for twelve and one-half years, had the vision to purchase the seven and one-half acres where the church is currently located. The first building to be erected on the property was a gymnasium, which was used for outreach to the community as well as a place of fellowship for church members. This ministry flourished under the leadership of Rev. Bob Shettler.

In 1977, the church called James Hammock as pastor; he was to lead the church for fifteen years. Under his leadership church membership grew to 1300. It was under Pastor Hammock's leadership that the church relocated to the present site. Also during the 1980's, Noah's Ark, a Christian childcare center was opened as a ministry of the church.

When Pastor Hammock resigned, the church was without a full time pastor for two and one-half years. In 1994, Dr. Gerald Robison answered the call to come to the church. He led the church for five years, and it was under his leadership that the church began Walk Through Bethlehem. Over the next thirteen years the church has presented Walk Through Bethlehem and has seen more than 130,000 people come through the "city".

In 1991, Pastor Robison resigned, and, once again, the church had to search for a pastor. In 2000, Rev. Chris Whaley was called as pastor. During the past eight years, Pastor

Whaley has led the First Baptist Church of Longwood to become involved in the FAITH evangelism strategy, which emphasizes church growth through the Sunday School. Pastor Whaley has also led the church to realistically deal with its debt and that debt has been reduced as a result of his leadership.

The First Baptist Church of Longwood continues to grow and reach out to the community. The church's emphases continue to be evangelism, Sunday School, missions, and "preparing the saints for a life of enduring commitment to Jesus Christ and lasting contribution to His kingdom… through worship, fellowship, discipleship, evangelism, and ministry" (Purpose Statement of the Church). In 2011, the First Baptist Church of Longwood celebrated 120 years of ministry.

Longwood Elementary School

This building located on Wilma Avenue was constructed in about 1883 and served until 1924 as the community school. It housed grades 1 – 8. In 1924, it was converted into the Longwood City Hall and Central Fire Department.

When the present City Hall was built in 1964 this building went into private ownership.

It was remodeled for use as a restaurant in the mid 1970's, but was extensively damaged by a fire in 1979. In 1984 it was modified for use as offices.

Longwood Elementary School 1923-1924
Grades 1-8

The Big Freeze of 1894-1895

Many early settlers came to Florida to invest in the citrus industry which blossomed after the Civil War. The Longwood area was no exception. With the development of the railroad into Central Florida, new markets for the enticing and exotic Florida fruit were opened up in the northeastern United States. By 1893, production had climbed to 5 million boxes and a large part of the population had a stake in the growth of the industry.

The Christmas season of 1894 was to change all of this unexpectedly and significantly. Christmas Day was typical, warm and sunny with temperatures hovering around eighty degrees. Three days later an extraordinary cold front arrived bringing with it unprecedented cold temperatures as low as 24 degrees. The Big Freeze had arrived!

Water pipes froze and burst and any of Florida's green vegetation that was not "cold hardy" turned black and died. The freeze lasted for 36 hours, which even today is uncommon. The citrus crop was an immediate casualty. The oranges, frozen solid on the branch, dropped off and rotted on the ground.

Even though many small growers were wiped out and had to return to the north, warmer weather in January brought hope for recovery for some. This hope was dashed, however, when a second freeze in February of 1895 brought even greater devastation. This time temperatures as low as 17 degrees killed not only the orange crop but the trees themselves. January 1895 had been warm enough to bring out the spring growth in the citrus and the trunks filled up with sap. The frozen sap expanded and burst the trunks of countless trees. Affected groves appeared to have suffered the affects of a forest fire. Production dropped to a mere 147 thousand boxes. As a result, growers, fearing similar catastrophes in the future, began the gradual process of moving the industry to locations further south in the state.

After the Big Freeze of 1894-1895, the area began to diversify agriculturally. Citrus made a slow comeback. Due to the lengthy replanting process, it wasn't until 1910-1911, that there was an equivalent post-freeze crop.

By 1915, production reached 10 million boxes. In the meantime, truck vegetables took up some of the slack along with cattle and small dairy farms. Tourism once again began to grow.

Section III

1895 – 1920

A slow recovery followed for the depleted population of the area. Not only was the citrus industry lost, but the area forests had been harvested by the saw mill. Some citrus was replanted. A small poultry business existed and tourists continued to arrive in smaller numbers each winter.

In 1913, Seminole County was carved out of north Orange County. Sanford was named the county seat.

The automobile made its appearance. Clay roads were paved, providing easier travel between Sanford and Orlando. Telephone service was now available and was followed by electric service in 1920. A local civic organization formed to encourage improvements in the appearance of Longwood. Social life revolved around the hotel and the Civic League building.

Articles

1. Longwood Civic League
2. Hon. M. O. Overstreet

The Longwood Civic League, Women's Club and Library

(A philanthropic and educational non-profit organization)

On December 28, 1911 a group of interested citizens met at the Longwood Hotel and organized the Longwood Improvement Society. Its purpose was to improve and contribute to the betterment of the town, as well as to fill a cultural need.

Their first project was cleaning the streets and placing barrels at convenient places for trash. Sawdust was bought and put on some of the roads. Petitions were drawn up, signed, and submitted to the town officials and the County Road Department. Clyde Clouser remembers, as a young boy, being assigned to light the new lanterns on the main street in the evenings. Clouser and his brother had the responsibility of making certain that there was enough oil in the seven street lamps to burn until midnight each evening. The Longwood Improvement Society had been headquartered in the old Masonic Lodge, but new regulations set forth by the building's owner forced the group to move. A building for the Society to use became a necessity.

On February 10, 1913, the members voted to change the name of their organization to the Longwood Civic League.

Also about 1913, Mr. Robinson of Sanford donated a lot on West Church Street and the League purchased the adjoining lot. Shortly after that, the West Longwood Chapel which was no longer in use was acquired for $50.00 with the stipulation that the building be moved. The building was located nearly a mile from town in West Longwood at the corner of Markham Road and Church Street, known as Stum's Corner.

Built in 1875 of rough hewn lumber this building is considered by most "Longwoodites" to be the oldest building in Longwood. The small vertically boarded building was known to boon time Longwood of the 1800's as the Self-Union Chapel. In addition to its function as a religious house, the Chapel also served as a meeting house and social gathering point for 19th century residents of West Longwood. Some people believe it was the first schoolhouse and meeting place built near its present location, then moved to West Longwood in about 1882. When the Big Freeze of 1894-1895 drove many settlers "back home", the Chapel, like the citrus groves, lay dormant, except for its occasional use as a dance hall or village theater.

In 1914, the Longwood Civic League purchased and moved the old West Longwood Chapel to its present location at 135 West Church Street in the heart of the Historic District of the city. The League enlisted the help of master carpenter Daniel Clouser in moving the building. Under Mr. Clouser's direction, mules and men successfully dragged the structure and set about renovating the 39 year old building. The renovations included the addition of a front porch and wings on both ends of the building. One wing contained a stage and an area that was soon used as a lending library. The wing on the other side provided additional seating space.

Soon the "Chapel" began to serve both as a meeting hall and a library. The library at one time included some complete volumes of Dickens, hand illustrated volumes of children's classics, and magazines published in the 1800's and 1900's. When Seminole County opened branch libraries in the Casselberry and Longwood areas in the late 1980's, the small library was closed and the books sold.

After its renovation, the building soon became a center for social activities including round and square dancing, plays, concerts, entertainment put on by the Longwood Tourist Group, bazaars, suppers, ice cream socials, and movies on Saturday nights. These activities brought the small community together.

Some of the people in attendance at early meetings recorded by signatures were: J.B. Clouser, George Dunbar, C.W. Entzminger, William Hartley, Adeline and J.A. Bistline, Walter Hand, Recording Secretary L. Dinkel, J.N. Searcy, F.J. Niemeyer, Frances, Mary and W.R. Healy and C.E. Walker, President. Although the gentlemen dropped out of the League after a few years, many of them continued to give counsel and assistance as needed.

The building served at the community's first schoolhouse and since has been a meeting place for clubs, churches, scouting groups, and weddings. During the late twenties and into the forties the League women met twice a month with one meeting devoted to making clothes and other articles that would be sold in the fall at their annual Bazaar and Dinner. Profits from this endeavor were sent to the Florida Children's Home in Jacksonville. The Civic League sponsored The Old Timers Reunion once a year for about 15 or 16 years in the 1980s and 1990s. These get-togethers were always very well received.

The League also put on a variety show called "Potpourri" for a couple of years at Lyman High School. It was directed by Elda Nichols. Singing, dancing, and skits were performed by members of the community and the League, including Aldia and Rayburn Milwee, Marion White, Rae Artmen, Charles Chapman, Carolyn Bistline, J.R. Grant, Bobby Hattaway and Slick Helms.

In 1998, the Longwood Civic League, now known as The Women's Club, thought that due to small membership and low funds the building should be sold. Instead, they decided to deed it to the Central Florida Society for Historic Preservation with the stipulation that it would someday become a museum. The Society renovated the building entirely and it still serves the community as the "Historic Civic Center c. 1880."

HON. M. O. OVERSTREET

Moses Oscar Overstreet was born in Kirkland, Georgia on October 10, 1869, the son of James W. and Susan Ann Solomon Overstreet. His father, who was in the agricultural and live stock industry, was a highly esteemed and influential citizen and lived to the age of 78 years. James was the father of fifteen children, all but one of whom lived to the age of maturity.

Moses Overstreet lived on the home farm until the age of 21. He then taught school for two years and later contracted to build railroad trestles and drains. He worked in the turpentine business with his brother-in-law with whom he came to Florida on September 16, 1898. He was engaged in the naval stores business in Orange County until 1923. He organized the Overstreet Turpentine Company with a capital of $200,000. From 1905 until 1917 he owned and operated a sawmill in Lockhart for the manufacture of fruit and vegetable crates under the name of Overstreet Crate Company. The company was capitalized at $200,000, employed 325 employees and turned out a million and a quarter crates annually. The mill burned in 1917. From that time, Mr. Overstreet was occupied in buying and selling land in Orange, Seminole, and DeSoto Counties. He was at one time the largest individual land owner in Orange and Seminole counties.

Mr. Overstreet moved from Plymouth to Orlando in 1903 and became president of the People's National Bank. He resigned his position in 1920.

He was active and influential in the affairs of city and county. He was a member of the Board of County Commissioners from 1907 until 1921. For the last 12 years of that period he was the chairman of the board. He was a member of the city council for a number of years and its president for two terms. In 1920, he was elected a member of the State Senate representing Orange, Seminole, and Osceola counties. He was re-elected in 1924.

Mr. Overstreet was a Mason, a Shriner, a Knight of Pythias, an Elk and a Moose. He married R. Ethelyn Chapman of Plymouth in 1900. Their children are Robert D., Hazel, Elizabeth and Mildred.

Section IV

1920 – 1930

This era began with the great land boom in the Miami area which then spread throughout Florida. Longwood's location between Sanford and Orlando made it an ideal location for attractions. Soon the area boasted the Seminole County Jockey Club with a grandstand and a mile long track. The Jockey Club was used as a winter boarding and training facility for race horses. The Longwood Hotel was a popular nightspot. A nearby golf course and the Sanlando Springs all together made Longwood a popular destination for central Florida residents.

Electric street lights replaced the kerosene lanterns at street intersections. A municipal water system was built to serve the small area of homes and businesses in the community. Several subdivisions were platted. Local roads that were paved included Longwood to Oviedo and Longwood to Markham. The road to Forest City and Apopka was paved as far as Sanlando Springs. A brick building housing a bank, drugstore, and barber shop replaced the wooden structures along East Lake Street across from the hotel. Gas stations and garages at the corners of West Warren and East

Lake Streets accommodated the growing automobile traffic between Longwood, Sanford and Orlando. The Black Bear Trail which became a section of the Old Dixie Highway passed through Longwood.

Articles

1. Joe Tinker and Walter Hagen
2. Frank Haithcox
3. Rolling Hills Golf Course

Joe Tinker and Walter Hagen

Joe Tinker was born in Mascoutah, Kansas on July 27, 1880. He was the son of Samuel and Elizabeth Williams Tinker. He started playing baseball as a rookie for the Chicago Cubs in 1902. He was an average hitter but a speedy runner. During this decade the Chicago Cubs went to the World Series four times and won the Series twice. He was best known as a shortstop.

A Tinkers-Evers-Chance combined double play was immortalized in the poem, "Baseball's Sad Lexicon". His incessant salary demands got him traded to the Cincinnati Reds. After a year playing and managing the Reds, he came to Florida where he scouted for and managed teams, and dabbled in real estate-- mainly in the Orlando area.

Longwood was experiencing a building boom in the mid 1920's. In 1925, Tinker built a business block at the junction of S.R. 427 and Church Street on the southeast corner. C.C. Jackson owned a grocery store there and Mr. Gray had a barber shop and grocery store there. Also, there was a bank on one corner. A cement block factory was also in town and by December, lots were being sold.

Deciding in early 1926 to capitalize on the golf enthusiasm of the area, the famed golfer, Walter Hagen was recruited to be president of a golf equipment company. By April 1926, their plant was operating making golf bags and they planned to add other articles for a full line of golf equipment. Joe managed the operation but Hagen was president.

Tinker Field Stadium, built in 1973 on a site where baseball had been played since 1914, was named for Joe. It is now part of the Citrus Bowl complex.

Joe married Mary Ross Eddington of Orlando in 1926. They had 1 son, Jerry. In a previous marriage there were four children, Joseph, Rolland, William and Ruby. Joe was an Elk and a Mason. He was inducted into the Baseball Hall of Fame in 1946, two years before his death on his 68th birthday, July 27, 1948.

Joe Tinker (left) pictured with St. Louis infielder Joe Stripp

Frank Haithcox

James Franklin Haithcox was born in Smith Grove, Davie County, North Carolina, May 7, 1882, the son of Daniel M. and Julia Ellen Heckard Haithcox. He was educated in the public schools of Winston-Salem, North Carolina.

Frank Haithcox's early life was spent in the theatrical profession. His biggest success was being in the original cast of "A Prince Pro-Tem" that had a record run at that time – the late 1890s – of nearly 200 nights in Boston.

Mr. Haithcox came to Orlando in 1921. He was involved in real estate projects in Longwood and developing beautiful Sanlando properties of Altamonte Springs. In 1927, Frank Haithcox opened the Sanlando Golf & Country Club, later named Rolling Hills.

Frank Haithcox organized five successful Florida corporations, among them the Orange Furniture Company which began business in 1923 under the able management of his father.

During World War I, he was attached to the staff of Major Woods at Explosive Plant Nitro, West Virginia. He was a member of the West Virginia four-minute-men (unattached) and headed up practically all Liberty Loan, YMCA and Red Cross work in that section. Mr. Haithcox's war work covered everything from isolated camps to convoy escort.

Frank Haithcox was a member of the Lion's Club, a Mason, and an Elk. He married Marion Day of Charlottesville, Virginia. They had 2 children, James Frank and Frances Amelia.

Reference: History of Orange County, Bachman, 1923

Rolling Hills Golf Course

The land which the Rolling Hills Golf Course now covers was adjacent to land homesteaded by the first resident of the area, Dr. Washington Kilmer, who arrived in 1872 and settled somewhere along what is now Raymond Avenue. He set out an orange grove which was probably abandoned after the big freeze of 1895.

In 1901, the Rolling Hills area, including Dr. Kilmer's holdings, was purchased by the Warnell Lumber Company. In 1906, Moses Overstreet bought half interest in the lumber company and the pine trees on the property were harvested for their gum resin. The resin was then distilled into turpentine in Mr. Overstreet's stills, one of which was located in the Longwood area. The pine trees were then milled and sold for lumber.

In 1922/23, suburbs were springing up and a large tract of land was acquired from Mr. Overstreet's company by Mr. Haithcox who was developing a subdivision he called Sanlando. It was on the northwest side of Altamonte Springs stretching all the way from Hoosier Spring, soon to be named Sanlando, on the north, south to Altamonte Springs and included the Rolling Hills area for which Mr. Haithcox mortgaged his company for $120,000.

Desiring a country club for his development of Sanlando, he contracted with Mr. Calvin O. Black, an experienced "golf man" from Cleveland, Ohio, to build it in return for 400 lots in the subdivision. Mr. Black contracted to build an 18 hole course, a watering system, and a clubhouse with foyer, dining room, golf shop, and men's and ladies' locker rooms. Before the end of 1926, life memberships had been sold to 3 prominent Altamonte Springs residents and as work progressed, more memberships were sold. Considerable interest was raised in 1928 when Mr. Hamilton Holt, president of Rollins College, and Dean Anderson joined the club. At this time, Mr. Black changed the name to Sanlando Springs Golf Properties.

The course was opened early in 1927, but dances were already being held every Wednesday night at the clubhouse. Highly dependent on the winter tourists in the area, the golf professional was only in residence during the winter months and spent his summers at another country club in New England. The dining room also closed during the summer. The golf course remained open to players all year. Sandwiches and drinks were available at a snack bar.

By 1930, with the Depression deepening, the Overstreet Development Company had foreclosed on the Haithcox properties and was operating the golf course as Sanlando Golf Properties in partnership with Mr. B.L. Maltby of Maitland.

In 1940, the property was sold to the Harris Brothers of Chicago, and some remodeling of the course was done. However, with the bombing of Pearl Harbor, the golf course was closed and for a few years after, the course was used as a cattle ranch.

In 1951, after 15 years of neglect, the Harris brothers sold the property to Harry Hutchinson and his wife, who changed the name to the Rolling Hills Golf Club in 1953. They sold the property in 1954 to the firm of Garapic, Kausek, and Lorbach, who immediately began to revive the golf course. In 1955, they sold the property to Art Hagen (no relation to Walter) who restored the course and built a new clubhouse.

In April of 1957, Hagen decided to lease the course back to Garapic, Kausek and Lorbach, doing business as "Gator Golf Inc.," who continued to improve the golf course, added a pro shop, a pool, and electric powered drinking fountains at both nines. The Lease-Purchase to Gator Golf was for 12 years with the provision that the lease could be bought out at any time during the 12 years.

At this point, Art Hagen made the greatest of his many contributions by offering to sell the property to the members to turn it into a private entity. This suggestion was ultimately decided in favor. To purchase the property, two corporations were formed: Rolling Hills Golf Course, a for-profit corporation, and Rolling Hills Country Club, a not-for-profit corporation. In February 1959, the agreement to secure the option was made. The next step was to finalize the purchase of the golf property from the Hagen family. This arrangement was made easier by the terms to which Mr. Hagen agreed in a new Lease-Purchase Agreement. It was a stretch for the club members, but on December 28, 1978, the club made its final payment to the Hagen family and the Rolling Hills Golf Course was now owned entirely by its members.

Over the years since, many improvements have been made. Gradual improvements to the course and building were made in 1987/88; the greens were completely rebuilt, enlarged, elevated, deepened and new ones created. In 1998, the club house received a complete remodeling to bring it into compliance with present day codes for handicapped personnel. The kitchen was also remodeled.

In 2002, the greens were again rebuilt to USGA standards, which was necessary to make the course competitive with newer courses being built in the area.

As of 2014, the course is lying fallow having been sold for eventual development.

References: A History of Altamonte Springs, Fl., 1920-1995, by Jerrell H. Shofner
A History of Rolling Hills Golf Club, 1926-1994 by Henry Kennedy
New Millenium Golf Growth Strategy. 2000

Section V

1930 – 1950

Longwood Elementary added four grades and became Lyman School. The Great Depression arrived in Longwood.

In December 1941, after the attack on Pearl Harbor, the war years provided employment for both men and women. Young men went to war and the military bases in the area provided many jobs.

Articles

1. Lyman School
2. George Barr Umpire School
3. E. Ruth Grant
4. J. Russell Grant

Lyman School

Home of the "Greyhounds"

The original Lyman School, located in Longwood, (today, Milwee Middle School), was built in 1923-24. It was named after Howard Charles Lyman. Mr. Lyman and his wife, Emma, were both New York entertainers who first came to perform for the winter guests at the Altamonte Hotel and Sanlando Country Club.

After Seminole County voted to separate from Orange County in 1913, Mr. Lyman won a seat on the School Board. Later, Mr. Lyman served on the local board of trustees for the bonding and building of schools in Seminole County and became a well known civic leader.

Construction of the new school began in 1924, but Mr. Lyman died a few days before the construction began. In appreciation of his work, the school was named after him.

Before Lyman was built, Longwood and Altamonte Springs were served by one room schools. Lyman opened in September 1924 with six rooms under the supervision of Howard C. Douglas. In 1926, it became an accredited junior high school under Herbert Chaffer, and six more rooms were added due to increased enrollment.

In 1932, Lyman served grades 1 through 12 for the first time. During the next few years, an auditorium was added as well as tennis courts and physical education changing facilities. W. J. Wells, Jr. served as principal c. 1941.

Rayburn T. Milwee, Sr. joined the Lyman faculty in 1939 as a teacher. The student population then was just over 200 students in grades 1 through 12. Mr. Milwee became principal of Lyman in1949 and was elected superintendent of schools for Seminole County in 1952.

Beginning in 1952, land east of the school was purchased and the road between the lake and the school was closed. A house on the land was used as a band room. The area experienced a post-war population explosion and new wings were added to the school. By 1956, the school housed only grades 7 through 12.

During the 1960's, improvements were made in the physical education facilities. At this time, the school principal was Ralph Diggs. A gymnasium was built and named for J. A. Bistline, a prominent civic leader in South Seminole County and a School Board member for 20 years.

Many more additions were built and Carlton Henley became principal in 1963 and remained in that position for 31 years. In 1967, Lyman was integrated and admitted its first black students.

In 1970, the school was moved to a new building one-quarter mile north of the old school. The old school became Milwee Middle School.

In 1994, Mr. Henley retired and was replaced by Dr. Peter Gorman. After 3 years, Dr. Gorman moved to Osceola and then to Orange County. Mr. Sam Momary became principal.

In 1999, Lyman celebrated its 75th anniversary. The year 2000 marked the first year of Lyman's new magnet program, the Institute for Engineering and Technology.

Sources: wikipedia.org/wiki/LymanHighSchool; "Images of America: Longwood"; www.lyman7576.com
     Milwee Middle School website

Lyman School - 1959

George Barr Umpire School

The George Barr Umpire School, established in 1935 in Hot Springs, Arkansas, moved to Orlando, Florida in 1947 for one year. In 1948, it was moved to the Sanford Naval Air Station in Sanford, Florida. The School operated for 6 weeks starting in mid-January.

During 1951, the Air Station was re-activated due to the involvement in Korea and the School moved to Longwood. Quarters were established in the Longwood Hotel, then owned and operated by Egie and Virginia Ward.

The School held its first session in Longwood in January and February of 1952. It operated there from 1952 through 1957.

The School then moved to Sanford, Florida to take advantage of the opportunity available in working with the New York Giants Baseball School. The School was established to make available to serious-minded young men the training and instruction required for working in professional baseball.

School personnel were invited by the Far East Command to be flown by Special Services of the United States Army to Japan to conduct training of United States Servicemen to umpire their vast baseball set-up.

The staff lectured and conducted classes in Japan, Korea, Philippines, Okinawa and Guam. Class was held also for Japanese Professional umpires. In 1951, the staff toured hospitals in Korea showing baseball and World Series films to service people.

Source: Eugene Bothell, Longwood, Florida

George Barr (center) with Gene Bothell (right) and Ward Mohs (left)

E. Ruth Grant

E. Ruth Grant moved to Longwood in 1945 with her husband, J. Russell Grant and their 3 children, Shirley, Sybil, and Frederick. Later, Richard and Patsy were added to the family.

Prior to marriage, Ruth Ansley Grant was active in church work, and her abiding faith led her into the ministry. A trailblazer for women in this field, Mrs. Grant became one of the earliest female ministers in the United Pentecostal Church in 1947. She was active in the formation of Pentecostal churches in Cassia, Belleview, Apopka, Orlando and Longwood.

Conducting prayer meetings in her home and in neighbors' homes, she started the First United Pentecostal Church of Longwood. She held Sunday school for Longwood's neighborhood children on Sunday afternoons, between regular church services when she pastored the Pentecostal Church in Apopka.

By 1958, the first sanctuary for the Longwood church was built at 561 E. Orange Avenue. Mrs. Grant continued to pastor and shepherd the church through congregational growth, and the enlarging of the facility. A larger sanctuary was completed in 1968.

Members of her congregation and many of Longwood's youth affectionately knew her as Sis Grant. Believing in the next generation, she poured time and love into working with young people. Weekly and monthly activities, as well as special events throughout the year, were planned for these adults-to-be.

Being a former teacher, she was eager to share her skills and talents without cost. Mrs. Grant would often tutor adults and children in academics, give Bible studies, teach music, and share her ability to play the guitar, accordion and piano. After 26 years, the Rev. Ruth Grant retired as pastor, but remained active another 20 years as Pastor Emeritus.

Her communication and organizational skills were used for a broad spectrum of services. She served as a PTA officer and the Homeroom mother who could be counted on for cupcakes and field trips. As the leader of a 4-H club, she taught sewing, crafts and cooking. The club members were often winners at county fairs and other competitions. She acted as taxi driver for the Little League games and Vacation Bible School. She served on city and county committees in various capacities. She was often asked to pray the dedicatory prayer at new Longwood businesses and other community functions.

Mrs. Grant served as campaign manager for her husband's political campaigns and often wrote campaign literature. For many years, she was the bookkeeper and secretary for Grant's Crawler Parts and Service, Inc., her husband's thriving business. During those 44 years, she dressed Santa Claus (Mr. Grant) for Longwood's annual Christmas party.

This gregarious and energetic lady loved people and Longwood. She earned the unofficial title of Fundraising Queen, always being available for school, band, city, church and many other worthy causes.

In 1986, Ruth Grant began researching the history of the Ansley family. Her research took her to England twice, and resulted in the publication of the book, "Hills of Ansley."

Quick to smile and offer southern-style hospitality, she made everyone welcome. Her coffee pot was always on and the door was always open-- no appointment necessary. She was there for you to share your joy or sorrow. After living in her beloved Longwood for 60 years, in 2005, she moved to a higher location.

Source: Sybil Grant Coombs

J. Russell Grant

As noted earlier, James Russell Grant, with his wife Ruth and children, moved to Longwood in 1945. The Grants quickly made friends and soon became involved in the community. When the Seminole County School Board wanted to close Lyman School and bus students, grades one through twelve, to Sanford for school, Grant was a leader among the residents that insisted Lyman School remain open.

In 1948, he formed a partnership with Frank Griffin, a friend and Longwood resident. Together they repaired bulldozers, draglines and other heavy equipment. Later, Grant formed Grant's Crawler Parts and Service. Inc. He maintained his bulldozer repair, welding and parts business until his semi-retirement around 1980.

Mr. Grant was deeply involved with the City of Longwood. Using his time and resources, he cleared the once dirt path that is now Grant Street with his tractor so people could get to the cemetery.

He was a volunteer firefighter and was involved in getting Longwood's first fire truck in 1950. Through the '60's and early '70's, he served on Longwood's Planning Board. He worked diligently to change Longwood's agricultural zoning to include residential, commercial, and industrial areas that would provide a better growth balance, and a secure tax base for the city.

His goal was to make Longwood a place where people could work as well as live. He wanted to see Longwood self-sufficient, having everything residents needed: jobs, hospital, bank, doctors and nursing home. At that time, the citizens of Longwood had to go to Sanford, Orlando or other cities to have these services.

When the City found itself in financial trouble in 1974, Mr. Grant ran for and was elected as a city councilman, and then Chairman of the Board. Since the City was financially strapped, he and Councilman Bud Scott persuaded the Council to serve without pay. He held the City Council/Commissioner seat from 1975 to 1985, and served as Mayor in 1984.

Mr. Grant was considered to be a progressive and stabilizing voice during his tenure. He was recognized for dealing effectively with the City's financial problems and streamlining and upgrading city departments. Critical infrastructure, including the water and sewer systems, were improved and expanded. The Police Department was upgraded, and a full-time Fire Department was implemented, with mandatory certification for all fire personnel. A second fire station was also constructed on the east side of the city, providing better protection for residents east of the railroad tracks.

Mr. Grant believed his greatest political accomplishment was attracting and getting South Seminole Hospital, and its adjoining Psychiatric Center, built on a former orange grove on SR 434. There was heated opposition over allowing the hospital complex to be built. Many residents wanted the developing city to remain a sleepy little town. The hospital has become a major asset for Longwood and its residents, and has provided many opportunities for employment.

In addition to city politics, Mr. Grant was active in civic and school activities. He was instrumental in getting lighting for the original Lyman High School football field. Without lighting, all night games were being played at other schools. Having no school allotment for band uniforms, he spearheaded getting Lyman's first uniforms, paid for by fundraising activities. He also built and donated the first batting cage for the baseball team.

He was the last surviving founder of what is now the Longwood-Winter Springs Chamber of Commerce.

One of his greatest enjoyments in the civic arena was being the city's Santa Claus for 44 years. He delighted children by arriving on a fire truck to hand out treats, and listen to their wishes for Christmas. He would go to nursing homes to delight and bring cheer to the residents.

In 2005, having lived sixty years in the city he loved, he died in the South Seminole Hospital. At his funeral, a proclamation was read proclaiming December 22nd as J. Russell Grant Day in the City of Longwood.

Source: Sybil Grant Coombs

Section VI

1950 - Present

During the 1950's Space Coast employment sparked home building on the east side of Longwood. With the completion of Interstate Highway 4 in the 1960's, new subdivisions expanded west along State Road 434. Longwood experienced a large growth in population. The Central Florida Society for Historic Preservation was founded. The historic district was identified, buildings authenticated, and the district was placed on the National Register of Historic Places.

Articles

1. The Central Florida Society for Historic Preservation (CFSHP)
2. Parkside Fellowship Church of the Nazarene
3. Northland – A Church Distributed
4. The Bradlee-McIntyre House
5. The Inside-Outside House
6. The Longwood Village Inn

The Central Florida Society for Historic Preservation

Perhaps no bigger Footprint has been left in Historic Longwood in the past 45 years than that left by the Central Florida Society for Historic Preservation (CFSHP). Chartered in 1969, it is now the owner of three restored historic buildings in the Longwood Historic District: the 1887 Bradlee-McIntyre House on Warren St., the Inside/Outside House (circa 1873), and the Old Civic Building (circa 1880)—both on Church St.

The society was chartered in 1969 by a group interested in restoring historic structures in East Central Florida using money grants obtained from a United States government program set up for this purpose. The badly vandalized Bradlee-McIntyre House on SR 436 in Altamonte Springs was the first house proposed by this group for revitalization. Unfortunately, before any work could be started, the government program was terminated. Unwilling to give up, several members convinced a number of like-minded people in the community of Longwood to proceed with work on the project. Among those attending the first meeting held in the Christ Episcopal Church were Mary McLeod, Dottie Pearson, Grace Bradford, Fred Bistline, Jo and Bob Hammond, Dick Bennett, Arthur Moore, Betty Woodruff, and Betty Brown from Orlando.

The participants were filled with commitment, but needed to raise money after it was decided to move the Bradlee-McIntyre House from its location on SR 436. The problem of a suitable location was solved with the donation of lots in Longwood by Bob and Grace Bradford. A sum of $5,000 was raised by sitting on the porch of the historic home and offering tours. Antique auctions, garage sales, and selling ice cream at the Lake Eola Craft Festival for two years still did not cover the cost of moving the Bradlee-McIntyre House to its new location in Longwood. Pressured by the current land owner of the existing site of the building, the group decided they would have to take the drastic step of borrowing the necessary money. Six dedicated members—Grace and Bob Bradford, Betty Jo McCleod, Dottie Pearson, Dick Venable, Myra Venable, and James Sutton took out personal notes to make up the $30,000 needed for the move. Dottie Pearson put up an additional $7,000 to move the Inside/Outside House from its location in Altamonte Springs and purchased a lot on Church St. for a new location for this unique historic building. Both buildings were moved in 1973. After two years, Grace Bradford took over the $30,000 loan from the bank. In the meantime grant requests were written to obtain money from the Florida Restoration Fund for both houses. A grant of $70,000, payable in installments over five years, was obtained for the Bradlee-McIntyre House. The grant application for the Inside/Outside house was apparently "lost".

Faced with paying off the loans, the Society decided to start a yearly Arts and Craft Show in Longwood. With cooperation from the City Council, the Arts and Craft Show became a reality. After two years of hiring a professional to manage the show, the members took on the job themselves and the show has continued to prosper to this day as an annual event held the weekend before Thanksgiving.

In time, the Society paid off the $30,000 mortgage and entered into a contract to buy the lot and repay the expenses incurred by Dottie Pearson for relocating the Inside/Outside

House. In the meantime, the Bradley-McIntyre House was furnished in late Victorian style and opened to the public. CFSHP Members continue to maintain the property and enhance furnishings through donations and acquisitions. Tours are facilitated by docents several times each month.

In 2000, the Longwood Civic League Building on Church St. was offered to the CFSHP and accepted with the condition that when the restoration was complete it would be used as a Museum of Longwood History. A grant for $20,000 was written to obtain money for the plans and cost estimates for restoring the building. It was granted, but when the grant for the money for the restoration was applied for, it was not approved. A reapplication was likewise unsuccessful. Using the plans obtained, the CFSHP moved ahead with restoration to the limits of society's financial ability. Recent updates included replacing the front porch and metal roof and updating the bathroom facilities. The building, now known as the Historic Civic Center, is currently used as a meeting place for civic organizations and churches, and is available for rental for small events. Funds generated from the rental of the building are used for maintenance and to continue preservation efforts.

The hard work and dedication of many members of the CFSHP over its forty-five year history have left a solid "Footprint in the Sands of Longwood".

Individuals interested in supporting the restoration and preservation of our historic landmark buildings are invited to visit the CFSHP website (www.cfshp.org) for current information about the Society, membership, volunteer opportunities or charitable contributions.

Parkside Fellowship Church of the Nazarene

The roots of Parkside Fellowship of the Nazarene are found in the Fern Park and Longwood Churches of the Nazarene.

Fern Park Church of the Nazarene was organized in 1957 and closed April 19, 2003. During its history, the church had many programs for the community and its members. The largest average attendance for Fern Park was in 1983 with an average of 63.

In May of 2002, Pastor Scott King came to the Fern Park Church. From 2002 – 2003, it was realized there was no room for expansion of the facilities of the Fern Park Church. The Longwood Church was struggling and the two congregations agreed to merge and utilize the Longwood church property.

The Longwood Church of the Nazarene was organized in 1957. Areva Barnes tells how the members worked every day and constructed the building themselves. The church grew through a bus ministry and community outreach. Over the years there were many programs implemented for church growth.

During one Sunday School drive, two girls rode their horses to church and gave the kids a ride.

The largest average attendance for the Longwood church was 155 in 1983. After a period of decline in membership and attendance, the Longwood Church agreed to merge with the Fern Park church and closed on April 19, 2003.

Parkside Fellowship Church of the Nazarene was organized on April 19, 2003. On this Easter Sunday, Fern Park Church of the Nazarene and Longwood Church of the Nazarene merged to become Parkside Fellowship Church of the Nazarene.

Source: Parkside Fellowship Church of the Nazarene, Longwood, Florida

Northland – A Church Distributed

In the early nineteen sixties, Northland Church was formed in the hearts of a handful of people. These folks learned how to share their faith, were trained in discipleship and follow up. They met on Friday evenings in private homes for Bible study, prayer and encouragement. This group quickly grew to approximately 200. After 3 years of discouraging results trying to bring a spark into their own church, they sensed the Lord calling them to begin a new church committed to evangelism, discipleship, and a spiritual multiplication.

Soon it was necessary to move from home meetings into a larger facility at the YMCA on Mills Avenue in Orlando. This church grew to several hundred on Sundays. God began leading 3 couples in the congregation to begin a similar church in the northern part of the city, thus Northland Community Church (NCC).

These couples first met in homes and then moved to school libraries. They sought a full-time pastor and grew from 60 to approximately 350 believers and established sister churches. From 1973 to 1974, NCC met in public elementary school cafeterias which required setting up and taking down each Sunday. Word got around Orlando that there was a non-traditional, Christ-centered church in Longwood. Part of the philosophy of the church at the time was never to become too large, own a building, or become too traditional in any way. However, with maturity and expansion, they began to see the need for a place to call their own. A building committee was formed and a new facility located – the old skating rink on Dog Track Road in Longwood.

Just before the move, the Lord led several to stay with the original philosophy of remaining smaller and beginning several satellites by sending out couples to start new churches. This group left and formed new churches. The remaining congregation, now cut in half, sought the Lord's direction and felt led to find a new pastor. Through a unique set of circumstances Dr. Joel C. Hunter was interviewed, unanimously accepted as God's choice for Northland Church, and re-ordained by Northland in 1985. Since that time the congregation has grown dramatically, and has added to and renovated the rat-infested skating rink. Even more important is the original vision, to bring Christians to a maturity which enables them to minister God's love, remains alive.

As the church continued to grow rapidly, extra church services were added. In the late '90's it was up to 7 services a week -- one being on Saturday night and Monday night and 5 services on Sunday. Neighboring land was purchased for parking from the Sanford Orlando Kenned Club on the south side of Dog Track Road. Newer and larger facilities were again needed and a ground-breaking service was held in November 2003. The church moved into the new facilities in August 2007. Total cost was $41.8 million. A cafeteria and bookstore are located in the main foyer. The word "Distributed" indicates the satellite churches in Mt. Dora, Oviedo, and West Oaks and more around the world.

Source: Northland, A Church Distributed

The Bradlee-McIntyre House

The 1880's were a pivotal time for the area presently known as Central Florida. Many of the towns in existence today had their beginning in that period of growth and expansion brought on in large part by the completion in 1880 of the South Florida Railroad extending from Sanford to Orlando (and eventually Tampa). Soon the area became popular with tourists and wealthy residents from northern cities who built large, Victorian homes, called them "cottages", and spent several weeks in the winter enjoying the appealing local climate.

In 1882, the Altamonte Land, Hotel, and Navigation Company was formed by a group of businessmen from Boston to build a town in Florida for wealthy Bostonians to spend the winter season. The Bradlee-McIntyre House, being part of this building boom, was originally constructed in Altamonte Springs near the railroad station, in the area of what is now Park Place and State Road 436. The Altamonte Hotel was opened in 1883 on Lake Orienta at what is now Maitland Ave and State Road 436. The luxurious hotel featured gas and water works and a street car line from the railroad station. One of Boston's leading architects, Nathaniel J. Bradlee, was commissioned to build several of the "winter cottages" so popular among the wealthy of the time. The cottage Mr. Bradlee built for himself, completed in 1887, has been one of the few to survive and has come to be known today as the familiar Bradlee-McIntyre House.

Mr. Bradlee was born into a wealthy Boston family in 1829. His career in civil engineering and architecture spanned several decades and involved the design of many iconic Boston landmarks. Included in his accomplishments are Greys Hall, which is one of three Victorian dormitories still standing in Harvard Yard, and the structurally significant 1860's Jordan Marsh building. A most notable challenge accepted by Mr. Bradlee was moving the seven-story Pelham Hotel several feet back on its lot to allow for street widening. The hotel weighed an estimated 10,000 tons.

Unfortunately, Mr.Bradlee and his second wife, Anna, enjoyed their "winter cottage" for only a brief period. In December 1888, he suffered a stroke aboard a train while on a business trip. In 1891, still owned by Mrs. Bradlee, the home was known as "Anna Villa" and hosted important social events including the marriage of distinguished local residents.

In 1893, U.S. Grant, Jr. rented the cottage for the season. The caretaker, Capt. N.H. Fogg had recently painted the cottage a canary color with white trim and green blinds. Newspaper accounts described it as "the most tastefully painted building in the county." The grounds were highly maintained featuring rare palms, roses, and orange trees laden with fruit.

Mr. Henry Green, of Cambridge, Massachusetts purchased the home in 1900. He further beautified the grounds, erected waterworks, and added a gas machine for lighting the house. Mr. Green had investments in timber land and sawmills in the area between Longwood and Sanford, and lumber from this area was transported to his lumber yards in

Boston. As was the custom among the wealthy winter residents of the time, the Greens entertained lavishly, decorating the twin parlors with vines, palms, and roses and inviting guests from all surrounding communities.

By mid-1904, the home's new owner, Mr. Maxwell S. McIntyre, planted a row of water oaks and added a new coat of paint to enhance his new property. A special variety of roses were procured from Germany. Mrs. McIntyre was a member of the Kellogg family and when the family arrived for the winter season, they were frequently accompanied by a large party of friends and guests. Sadly, in 1905, a guest who came to visit the McIntyres hoping to improve his health in the warm Florida climate, passed away. His funeral was held in the parlor.

In 1906, Mr. McIntyre purchased the Altamonte Hotel and planned extensive improvements to that property as well. Mr. McIntyre, being interested in building up the entire area into a "charming tourists resort", contributed to various church and public improvements. When the McIntyres decided to live year round in Altamonte Springs, they added a summer kitchen and bath connected to the rear of the house by a breezeway. This was necessary as the original house had no kitchen because previous owners had relied on the catering service from the Altamonte Hotel.

After the death of Mrs. McIntyre in 1946, the house passed through several owners and began to deteriorate. It was eventually abandoned. When the City of Altamonte Springs wanted the land for development, the house was offered for sale for $1.00 provided the buyer could move the house to a new site. If no buyer came forward, the house was to become the victim of a fire-fighting exercise by the fire department.

Fortunately, the newly formed Central Florida Society for Historic Preservation came to the rescue. The group recognized the value of saving this rare remaining example of Victorian architecture and reminder of a past genteel era so different from life in Central Florida today. The group hoped to use government grants to accomplish their mission. Unfortunately, before any work could be started, the government program was terminated. The group was successful in raising private funds, and in 1971, the house was moved to its present location in Longwood and preserved for local citizens to enjoy a peek back into that bygone era of early Florida.

The Inside-Outside House

The Inside-Outside House was moved to its present location in Longwood from Altamonte Springs in 1973. Its name, Inside-Outside House, derives from the fact that the studs are placed on the outside in order that the interior walls would be smooth and require no plaster or trim.

The house was built by sea captain W. Pierce near Boston in 1870. It was constructed as one of the first prefabricated buildings. The downstairs was to be used as a cabinet shop—cabinet making had long been a passion of the Captain—and the upstairs was to be used as living quarters. In 1873 the house was dismantled and shipped to Jacksonville. From there it travelled up the St. Johns River and then by mule cart to Altamonte Springs. The Captain re-erected the house on government land after consulting with government officials. He was to return to Florida in 1878 and purchase 100 acres of land surrounding the house for the price of $100.00. In the meantime, the house was to be used as a rest stop and field station for federal soldiers and their horses.

In late summer of 1878, the Captain retired from the sea and returned to Florida with his wife, his tomcat Brutus, tools, and a large quantity of lumber. He paid the government $50.00 of the agreed purchase price with the remaining $50.00 to be paid in 1881. The house was to be available to soldiers for lodging in lieu of his paying interest on the balance. In 1881, when he was unable to pay that balance, his wife's brother from Boston bought the property with the understanding that the Captain and his wife were to be allowed to live in the house until they both died. The land ownership changed many times but the Pierces continued to live in the house until their deaths.

Originally there was an outdoor stairway, but later the Captain built an inside stairway patterned after a ship's ladder. He is also credited with the upstairs fireplace mantel. Later owners built the downstairs fireplace and plastered the walls, added the porch, and changed the orientation of the house.

The Captain continued to work as a cabinet maker and is believed to have worked on the Altamonte Hotel and the Bradlee-McIntyre house, even though business was frequently bad. In an era when the population of the area known as Central Florida was limited, he made many friends and was popular from St. Cloud to Sanford due to his experiences at sea and his congenial personality. He suffered from rheumatic pains in his legs which he claimed were better in Florida than either at sea or in Boston. Mrs. Pierce is remembered as an expert cook who was willing to fix meals for anyone who came by, regardless of the time of day.

Brutus, the tomcat that accompanied the Captain to sea and on the move to Florida, was his constant companion for 17 years. The death of Brutus was very traumatic for the Captain. The last "masterpiece" the Captain built was a coffin for Brutus which was said to be "a coffin fit for a king". The death of the favored tomcat seemed to change the Captain. His health seemed to suffer and he spent the last part of his life in bed.

The exact date of the Captain's death is not known, but for many years after, the house was the home of Dr. Christy, an early nematode expert.

As land increased in value in the 1960's and early '70's, the house fell into disrepair and was threatened with destruction. Using private funds, it was moved, along with the Bradlee-McIntyre House, intact, from the site on Boston Avenue in Altamonte Springs to Longwood in 1973. Restoration followed. It now houses the Cottage Gift Shop.

The Longwood Village Inn

The large Victorian building which today stands in the center of Longwood's Historic District has had a rich and varied existence, mirroring the ups and downs of this part of Florida where it has stood for more than 130 years.

In 1883, E.W. Henck, president of the South Florida Railroad Company and founder of Longwood, commissioned Josiah B. Clouser to build a hotel. Clouser was well known for constructing Victorian Homes in what is now known as Central Florida. The hotel, named "The Waltham", was completed by 1888. The structure was a wooden "cracker" style building with Victorian details. Large porches provided shade and ventilation. Twin fireplaces on opposite sides of the building warmed the two dining rooms and the lobby. There were indoor bathrooms on each floor and electric bells. The rate per day was $3.00.

Longwood, with its new hotel and fine citrus groves was a thriving village. Henck named the town after a suburb of Boston which he had helped lay out on an estate known as Longwood previously owned by David Sears. Sears chose the name for his estate originally due to his fascination with Napoleon whose home during his exile on St. Helena was called Longwood. Hence, the small village in the nearly uninhabited heart of Florida was linked in a very tenuous and indirect way to the Emperor Napoleon.

Tourists were drawn to Longwood and the surrounding area for its sulphur springs and the celebrated hunting and fishing in the area. Some rode on Henck's railroad, later incorporated into the Seaboard Coast Line. Others ventured down from Jacksonville by steamboat on the St. Johns River to Sanford and then continued by horse and wagon. Regrettably, the winter of 1894-1895 and the unprecedented freeze that accompanied it were devastating for Longwood and the surrounding area. Groves, as well as the crops that year, were destroyed. The economy was shattered and tourism was nearly at a standstill. Like many buildings and homes, the hotel was empty and closed until C.W. Entsminger, a Florida legislator, purchased and refurbished the hotel in 1910 as the economy began to recover. Among other improvements, Entsminger added gaslights to the lobby—innovative for the time.

In 1922, Entsminger sold the hotel to George E. and Florence Clark who renamed it the St. George Hotel. By then Florida and Longwood were once again booming. The new highway, Route17-92, by-passed the hotel, but the Dixie Highway still ran in front and the train station was across the street. The hotel acquired a new fence that discouraged any unrestrained cows and other livestock. Soon fence ordnances were passed that also helped do this job.

Unfortunately, tragedy was to accompany these new endeavors. In 1923, The Clarks, who were very active in civic affairs, were honored with a special gathering. During the party Mrs. Clark noticed the absence of her husband. Going to look for him, she found him in a small building behind the hotel. He had met with an accident. Sadly, his death occurred the following day. (Mr. Clark is rumored to be the elusive "ghost" who has been reported to haunt the building today.   According to Shadowlands Haunted Places Index, there is a presence that moves around the third floor at night, turning lights off and on and operating the elevator. One story tells of the police responding to a burglary call and seeing someone in a third floor window. A room-to-room search found nothing. Many believe that George Clark is still protecting his hotel!)

Mrs. Clark leased the hotel to her brother-in-law Fred A. Clark, who renamed it the "Orange and Black". The hotel, perhaps due to its rural location between Sanford and Orlando, became one of the finest gambling establishments in this part of Florida. Bookies were in the north end of the building and the games of chance were played in what would be the main dining room.

In 1926, Ed Crocker, head of a syndicate which included baseball great Joe Tinker, took over the hotel. Repainted and renamed, the Longwood Hotel was again noted for its southern charm and hospitality. Indicative of this, in 1924, the National Governors' Conference met in Jacksonville and visited sites throughout the state in touring cars. After a stop in Sanford, the group arrived at Longwood and paused at the Longwood Hotel.   Longtime resident, Mr. John Bistline offered cigars to the men and coffee to the women. There was a short address by both the governor and mayor and the group continued their tour on to Maitland. *(There are varying versions of the date and the events of the visit by the governors, but this version originates from John Bistline Jr. as he remembers it being told by his father.)*

With the depression in the 1930's, along with nearly all of Florida, the Longwood Hotel experienced a decline. U.S.O. dances were held in the ballroom until the new owner F.S. Sanders removed the dance floor in 1946.

Change came again in 1947 when Maximillian Shepard, a restaurateur, purchased the Hotel. He advertised wisely and attracted several conventions. Mr. Shepard's restaurant was famous all over Central Florida for its cole slaw and southern cooking.

George Barr, a well-known National League umpire for 19 years, conducted the George Barr Umpire School at the Hotel from 1952-1957. A row of shower stalls was built across the back of the building to accommodate the athletes.

In the meantime, Shepard auctioned the hotel to L.T. Hunt, Sr. Mrs. Hunt, who had been married in the hotel, ran the restaurant and lived in an apartment on the second floor. When she died, ownership went to her son, L.T. Hunt, Jr., who ran the hotel as a low rent boarding house for migrants.

In 1966, the movie *Johnny Tiger* (originally called *The Cry of the Laughing Owl*) with Robert Taylor, Chad Everett, and Linda Scott, was partially filmed in the hotel.

In 1969, the Central Florida Society for Historic Preservation selected Longwood as the nucleus of its historic preservation efforts. The Longwood Hotel was the hub of the plan. Grace Bradford, member of the Society, purchased the hotel in 1972 and changed the name to the Longwood Village Inn. The purchase price was $85,000 and $65,000 was put into restoration. Mrs. Bradford's first step was to have to all the boarders move out. Next she removed the trash, weeds, old trucks, ramshackle shacks, and shower stalls remaining from the umpire school. The Bradford's then began the actual renovation work in November of 1972. Their grand opening party was held January 2, 1973.

The lobby of the Inn was decorated with Victorian antiques, and two dining rooms served as many as 300 meals a day. Part of the ground floor was used for banquets, private parties, and wedding receptions. Two or three wedding took place on the stairs of the lobby. Governor Reuben Askew was one of many distinguished visitors to the Inn during the Bradford's brief ownership.

In 1973, Mr. and Mrs. Georges St. Laurent, Sr., of Clauster, New Jersey bought the hotel for $225,000. Their daughter Carrie and son-on-law, Spyros Christoulatos, managed the restaurant and converted the second dining room into a country and western bar. Also added, replacing the old garden, was a Greek-style walkway to the parking area in the rear. Now the hotel, with an old carriage found in Tampa outside, and the rediscovered pine floor with its extra-long planks used as a dance floor, was again the scene of weddings and parties. Chandeliers with Grecian touches and Tiffany-styles helped set the atmosphere. Believed to be original, a four-sided seat in the center of the lobby was accented by a fireplace topped by a beveled glass mirror.

On July 25, 1976, due to the efforts of Mrs. Bradford, the Florida Bicentennial Committee dedicated the Longwood Village Inn as a Historical Landmark along the Bicentennial Trail. It was the first such site named in Florida.

In 1978, when Mr. St. Laurant, Sr. died, his wife donated the hotel to Cornell University. The University leased the hotel offices and restaurants to several different managers after acquiring ownership. A private investor fund named Longwood Village Investors, Ltd. purchased the Inn from Cornell 1983. They completed major renovations in the mid 1980's converting the property to offices. It continued to operate as offices and executive suites until sold to the present owner, also a private investment group, Homevest Properties, LLC in 2006. At present (2014), the Longwood Village Inn remains a successful office complex. Improvements, inside and out, continue.

Made in the USA
Las Vegas, NV
04 March 2022

44955937R00037